www.trafford.com

North America & international
toll-free: 1 888 232 4444 (USA & Canada)
fax: 812 355 4082

A *Diva's* EXPRESS GUIDE TO ENTERTAINING

LUTHERIA HOLLIS

Three generations of Divas

A Diva's Express Guide to Entertaining is my ideas and expressions on Parties and Events.

I guess I inherited the creative gene and I have a great palate as well. I also have a creative eye. I am often asked my opinions and ideas on events.

This book is some of my ideas about entertaining with a few of my recipes added in for your enjoyment.

SPICE IT UP

Every Woman should make sure they have the right spices in their kitchen cubbards at all times.

The secret to a good cook is to know how to "Spice it up" but the Secret to a great cook is having what you need when you need it.

Here is just what you need on the shelves and a variation there of:

Lawry's Seasoning Salt

Lawry's Parslied Garlic Salt

Kosher Salt

Black Pepper (Different Coarseness)

White Pepper

Lemon Pewpper

Red Pepper Flakes

Ground Thyme

Sage

Sazon

Chicken Boullion Cubes

Corn Starch

Baking Powder

Lipton Onion Soup Mix

Garlic Aioli

Hot Sauce

Lemon Juice

Cinnamon

Nutmeg

Powdered Sugar

Asian Sesame Salad Dressing (great as a marinade for fish and a sauce for it too!)

Raspberry Dressing

Ginger Dressing (great for salads and for sauce and marinades)

Dale's Steak Seasoning (Low Sodium) – The Best Steak Marinade. Use your Grill Pan and you are good to go!

Garlic Powder,

Onion Powder,

Creole Seasonings,

Italian Seasonings,

Celery Salt,

Blackened Seasonings,

Browning Sauce,

Cloves,

Mojo Marinade

COCKTAILS ANYONE?

Every Diva makes sure her guest are served according to their preferences.

Make sure you have on hand the Basics at your Home Bar.

VODKA	TEQUILA
GIN	LIGHT RUM
SCOTCH	DARK RUM

And don't forget the Mixers

CLUB SODA	GINGER ALE
TONIC WATER	THE JUICES
COKE	TRIPLE SEC
DIET COKE	

Now my favorites are the Wines. Everyone's taste is Wines is so varied but having a nice selection will make you the hit of your party, here is just some ideas:

CHARDONNAY	PINOT GRIGIO
MERLOT	MOSCATO
ROSCATA	CHAMPAGNE (my personal favorite)

ROSCATO

Now Divas, nothing makes a drink better than how it is served. Make sure you have all the proper glasses. This is so important. It is like the dress, without the hairdo- you feel me.

They don't have to be expensive. Make sure you have the different colors, shapes, styles.

Beer glasses, Martini glasses, champagne flutes, wine glasses and water/soda glasses.

Several glasses can serve multiple purposes. And Divas- Don't forget to garnish your drinks.

***Diva Tip:** Stores like Marshalls, TJ Maxx and Home Goods have a variety of types and styles of glasses that are Fabulous and at great prices.

Lutheria's Apple Martini

1 oz Green Apple Vodka

½ oz Sour Apple Schnapps

½ oz Midori

½ oz Apple juice

½ tsp sugar optional

Ice cubes

Martini shaker

Martini glass

Green apple slice for garnish

Mix all ingredients into Martini shaker. Shake until mixed. Pour into Martini glass.

Garnish with apple slice. Serve.

Pomegrante Sangria

48 ounces Cran-Pomegrante Juice

16 ounces of Orange juice or Orange Juice Blend

24 ounces Pineapple Juice

3/4 cup of Sugar (add more to taste)

2 shots of Cointreau Liquer

100 ml of Brandy

Fruits to Garnish - Blackberries, Chopped Apple, Mandarian Oranges, Orange Slices

Mix all ingredients together in a bowl. Stir until mixed well. Taste and add additional sugar if needed. Know your audience, if they prefer more alcohol add more brandy, if they like it sweeter add a little more sugar. Serve over ice and garnish with fruit. This is a great Holiday drink and great at parties.

Red Wine Sangria

1 bottle Red Wine

I can frozen limeade (prepare according to directions)

I large bottle pineapple juice

1 can frozen orange juice (prepare according to directions)

½ cup sugar

Grapes

Orange slices

Ice cubes

Mix well first 5 ingredients in a pitcher. Serve individual glasses over ice, garnish with grapes and orange slice

Basic Mimosa

Ingredients:

- Champagne
- 2 oz. cold orange juice
- Orange slices for garnish (if using large wine glass)
- Crushed ice (optional)

Preparation:

Pour orange juice into a champagne glass, add champagne to fill, and garnish.

Variations:

- Add a table spoon of Grand Marnier and you'll have created a Grand Mimosa
- Use cranberry juice instead of orange juice and enjoy a Lilosa
- A fauxmosa is a virgin mimosa (no champagne). Use 7up or sprite in place of champagne

White Wine Sangria

Ingredients:

- 1 Cup pineapple juice
- 1 Cup white grape juice
- 1 Cup peach nectar
- 1 Bottle white wine
- 3 Tbs. lemon juice
- ¼ Cup sugar
- Lemon and lime slices

Preparation:

Combine wine, fruit juice, and sugar in pitcher. Add ice cubes and stir until very cold. Garnish with slices of lemon and lime

GAME NIGHT

Thinking of Hosting a Game Night Party or Board Games?

What do I serve?- Try serving Casual Fare for this Easy Breezy Night.

*** **Diva Tip:** Don't Over do it. Serve "Easy Handlers"
Like the Conch Fritter or Conch Salad and Cocktails
TABOO anyone?

Lucy's Conch Fritter's

1 fresh conch

1 tomato

1 medium onion

1 green bell pepper

1 red bell pepper

1 bunch Fresh Thyme

1 goat pepper

2 cups of self rising flour

1 tablespoon of baking powder

3 tablespoons of tomato paste

2 cups of water

2 cups of vegetable oil

Salt

Wash conch in a bowl with salt and vinegar. Slice into small chunks. Slice tomato into small chunks. Slice onion into small chunks. Slice green and red bell peppers into small pieces. Mix conch and all vegetables into a bowl. Add thyme without stems into the mixture along with tomato past, baking powder and flour. Stir in water and mix into a batter. Add salt to taste. Slice goat pepper into very tiny pieces then add to taste. Heat deep fryer to 350 degrees. Use a tablespoon to drop batter into deep fryer. Turn fritters until light brown all over.

Makes two dozen or more servings.

Lucy's Bahamian Conch Salad

1 fresh conch

1 half ripen tomato

1 small onion

2 celery stalks

1 green bell pepper

1 red bell pepper

1 goat pepper

3 limes

Salt

Wash conch in a bowl with salt and vinegar. Slice into small chunks. Slice half ripen tomato into small chunks. Slice onion into small chunks. Slice celery into small pieces. Slice green and red bell peppers into small pieces. Mix conch and all vegetables into a bowl. Cut limes into halves and squeeze into mixture. Add salt to taste. Slice goat pepper into very tiny pieces then add to taste.

Makes 4 to 5 small servings.

This is my very good friend Lucy recipe. She also makes a mean Conch Fritter. Those Bahamian Girls can cook.

No More Plastic Plates!!!!!

I know my daughters are laughing like crazy as they are reading this.

When entertaining your guest, please Divas, do not serve them on plastic plates.

Dinner plates are so cost effective these days, you can purchase a 16 piece set or individual plates at stores like Marshalls, Ross, TJ Maxx, etc. Even Family Dollar. You can mix and match.

You can use Plain, Colored and Patterned napkins and you have created a beautiful and unique table each and every time.

I will never forget, Oprah's party planner Colin Cowie said it best- He creates a dinner party every night. He has to eat. Whether it's a dinner for two or 12 set the table and eat!!!!

***Diva Tip:** Some Party Supply & Equipment Rental Stores often sell leftover inventory once a year. This includes Dinnerware, Cutlery and Glassware.

Breakfast Casserole

1 ½ lbs of Bulk sausage

9 eggs

3 cups of milk

3 slices of bread

1 ½ cups of shredded cheddar cheese

Salt or seasonings

½ tsp of dry mustard

Brown and crumble sausage in skillet. Drain.

In a bowl, mix eggs, milk, salt and dry mustard together. Add cheese and crumbled up bread slices and sausage to egg mixture.

Pour mixture into well greased 13" X "9 pan. Cover and leave overnight.

Bake at 350 degrees for 40 minutes covered, then additionally for 20 minutes uncovered. Cut into squares and serve.

Hashbrown Breakfast Casserole

Country Style hashbrown shredded potatoes (10 oz)

8 ounces container sour cream

Sliced shallot onions (regular can be substituted)

Colby Jack Cheese (8 oz or more)

Lawry's Seasoning Salt

Milk (¼ cup)

2 eggs

Saute onions in butter until limp. Add onion to bowl with shredded potatoes, add eggs, sour cream, cheese and seasonings. Add milk. Mix thoroughly. Add mixture to greased baking pan.

Bake at 400 degrees for approximately 45 minutes. Check after 30 minutes, then 15 minutes later. Cut into the mixture to check for doneness. Cook for additional few minutes if nedded. Serve

Queche'

9 inch pie crust

1/2 cup of mayo

½ cup of milk

2 eggs

1 tbs of corn starch

½ tbs cooked bacon

(Crumbled ham, crab meat or spinach optional)

1 1/3 cup of shredded sharp cheddar cheese or swiss

1/3 chopped green onion

Mix together all ingredients and spoon into 9 inch deep dish pie pan. Bake at 350 Approximately 35-40 minutes until firm.

*May add mushrooms if desired

Pasta Primavera

Penne Pasta

½ box frozen chopped spinach (defrosted)

1 can Rotell tomatoes with green chiles

½ box frozen vegetables (defrosted)- this should in include the vegetable you like, brocolli, cauliflower, carrots are the usual mix.

½ green pepper sliced

½ large onion –sliced

1 jar of Classico Sundried tomatoe Alfredo Pasta Sauce

Feta cheese

Red Pepper flakes

Garlic Salt

Saute onion and green peppers in a little olive oil until crisp. Add chopped spinach to saute, turn along the way. Allow to cook about 3 minutes, add red pepper flakes. Now this will depend upon your taste, "Some like it hot". Add chopped frozen vegetables. You may want to chop these a little finer than the way they come in the box. Makes a better pasta dish. Add your chopped tomatoes and Garlic Salt. Simmer for about 5 minutes until a little saucy but not dry and not watery.

Boil your Pasta. Drain. Add vegetable mix to Pasta. Mix thoroughly. Pour Classico Sauce over entire mixture, turning and coating and mixing. Add Feta cheese. Return to heat foe about 3 minutes. Taste, plate and serve.

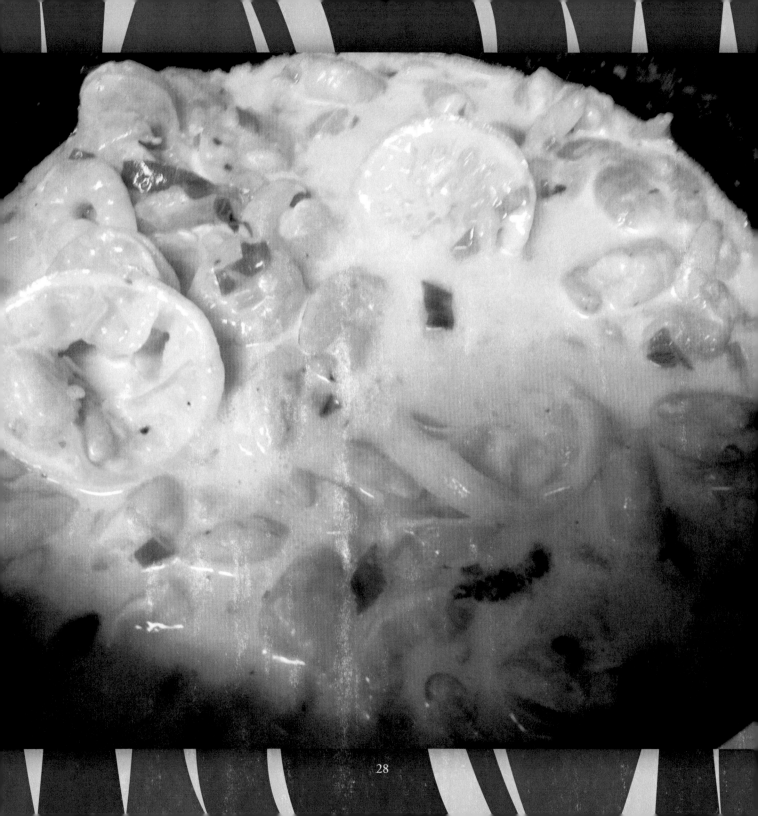

Shrimp Scampi

1 pound medium of peeled/deveined shrimp

Lemon juice

2 fresh lemons, juiced

3 cloves of garlic

1 bunch of green onions (sliced up to scallion top)

1 stick of Butter

Lawry's Parslied Garlic Salt

Season your shrimp with garlic salt. Melt butter and green onions in a saute pan until slightly crisp. Add pressed garlic to pan. Add juice of 2 lemons. Taste your sauce. Add your shrimp. Do not overcook shrimp, should take about 4 minutes , depending on how well done you prefer your shrimp. Add additional garlic salt and lemon juice to your taste, make sure there is enough sauce. Serve over Angel hair pasta. Garnish with Lemon Slices.

**** **Diva Tip:** I sometimes add fresh tomatoes and make it A la Fresco.

Fish with Coconut Sauce

4 tilapia fillets or red snapper fillets

2 tbsp. olive oil

3 cloves fresh garlic, minced or pressed

1 medium white onion, chopped

1 chopped green pepper

3 tbsp. tomato paste

1 can of coconut milk

1 Chicken Bouillon cube

2 cups cooked white rice (hot)

Season fish to taste. Set aside. Saute onions , green pepper and garlic in olive oil. Add chicken bouillon cube. Then add in tomato paste blending in. Shake up coconut milk making sure well mixed. Add to sauté mix. Add additional seasonings of your choice. Add fillets to cook in mixture, do not let fall apart, choice to doneness. Coating with sauce. Serve over rice.

Salmon Stir Fry

lb. Norwegian Salmon

package of Asian vegetables with Roasted cashews

Asian Sesame Salad dressing

1 small onion sliced

clove of garlic- pressed

tbsp. Olive oil

Red Pepper flakes

Salt

Pepper

Brown Salmon on both sides in deep frying pan with Olive oil. Add sliced onion and pressed garlic.

Add Asian Vegetables mix on top. Add Red pepper flakes. Salt and Pepper for your taste. Pour ½ bottle of Asian Sesame dressing on top of entire mixture, enough to coat and make a sauce. Simmer for approximately 10 minutes on Medium heat. Serve over Jasmine Rice. A Green Salad would top this off.

Honey Curry Chicken

12 pieces of chicken (all dark or mixed)

Curry powder

Lawry's seasoning salt- to taste

Black Pepper- to taste

2 jars of Country Dijon mustard

2 small jars of honey

Season chicken well with seasoning salt and pepper. Sprinkle with curry powder. Coat well. Mix in a seperate bowl the Mustard and honey, this will be your marinade. Stir together well.

Dip each piece of chicken in marinade and lay in your large baking dish. After each piece is coated. Cover and bake at 375 degrees for 30-40 minutes until well cooked. If you are not sure, check with you meat thermometer.. Pour remaining marinade over chicken. Turn oven up to 400 degress, uncover, Bake approximately 10 minutes until golden brown. The remaining juices mixed with marinade will make a delicious gravy for chicken.

*** **Diva Tip:** Serve this dish with Jasmine Rice and a Green Vegetable. Great for a Small dinner party or just to mix it up for a family dinner.

Palermo Pasta

Ingredients:

- ½ lb. bulk Italian sausage
- 1 lb. medium peeled deveined shrimp
- 1 Bunch sliced green onions
- 1 Large zucchini sliced thin
- 1 Large (16oz) heavy cream
- 8 oz. shredded parmesan cheese
- 1 Chicken bouillon cube
- 1 Box angel hair pasta
- Tony Chachere's Famous Creole's Seasonings

Preparation:

Season shrimp with creole seasoning. Brown Italian sausage with green onions and then drain. Add heavy cream, chicken bouillon cube and zucchini to mixture. Add additional seasonings to taste. Cook approximately 10-15 minutes over medium heat. Add shrimp and simmer until cooked. Add cheese until thickened and serve over angel hair pasta.

Marinaded Steak

1/2 cup Balsamic Vinegar

1/2 cup Barbeque Sauce

1/2 Cup Dale's Marinade

(This is enough for 3 average steaks)

Lightly season steaks if you like, I personally do not add any seasoning to my steaks when using this marinade. Add steaks to large Freezer bag with Ziploc, add above ingredients.

Leave in Refrigerator overnight. Place on grill or grill pan, cook to desire temperature. Perfecto!

Lutheria's Sweet and Sour Meatballs

Ingredients: (Can be doubled)

- 1 Bottle of chili sauce
- 1 Can of whole berry cranberry sauce
- 1 One pound bag of beat meatballs

Preparation:

Pour into a large sauce pan, the chili sauce and cranberry sauce. Melt and let simmer. Add meatballs and let them coat, simmer for 10 minutes.

For Parties: transfer to a crockpot. Have on hand an extra-long extension cord and you can set it up anywhere and this will be a hit all day or night long.

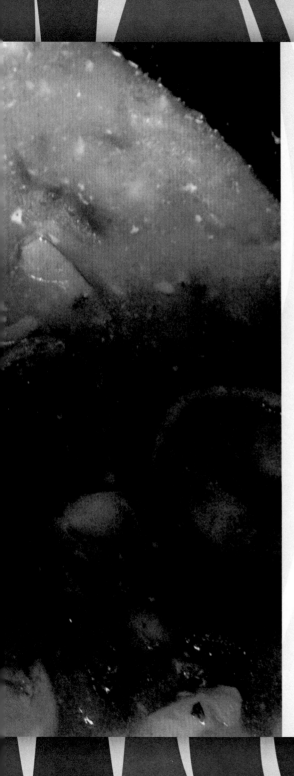

Easy Jambalaya

1/2 pound of Shrimp

1 pound of chicken breast - cut in pieces

2 links of Andouille sausage sliced

1 can of Roteille tomatoes- mild

1 can of chicken stock

1 package of cut frozen Seasoning blend (onions, celery, green peppers)

1 tbsp flour

Creole Seasonings

Saute and Cook Chicken, sausage and seasoning blend in saucepan. Add tomatoes and chicken stock. Reserve 1/4 cup and mix with flour to make a roux. Mix Roux and add to mixture. Cook for 25 minutes. Season shrimp with Creole seasoning and add to saucepan 5 minutes before end of cooking time. Serve over Rice. O la la!!!!!!

Turkey Chili

1 pound of ground Turkey

1 can of Black Beans

1 can of spicy Pinto Beans

1 can Rotele mild Tomatoes

1 packet of Chili-O Seasoning Mix

1 onion-chopped

Brown Ground turkey and onion. Add Black Beans, drain a little. Add Spicy Pinto Beans.

Add Tomatoes, then Seasoning Mix. Simmer for approximately 20 minutes. Serve in bowl with a little cheddar cheese on top if desired. Maybe be Caliente!!!!!

Vegetarian Eggplant Lasagna

Ingredients:

- 2 c. pasta sauce
- ½ tsp. Italian seasoning
- ¼ tsp. basil
- ¼ tsp. parsley
- 1 lg. eggplant, sliced in circles
- 1 c. Ricotta cheese
- 4 oz. Mozzarella shredded cheese
- 4 oz. Shredded Italian cheese mix (publix)

- 1 Box lasagna
- 1 Bag Bird's Eye frozen onion and pepper mix

For Breaded Eggplant:

- 2 Egg yolks
- ½ c. all purpose flour
- ½ c. Italian bread crumbs
- Mix Italian seasoning and salt as preferred

Preparation:

About an hour before starting, set up paper towels on a large flat dish and layer eggplant slices sprinkled with salt. Use many paper towels, then cover with heavy object (this will help dry out water from eggplant so they can be crispy after baking).

After drying eggplant slices, beat egg yolks in bowl. Dip eggplant in flour, egg yolk, and then bread crumbs. Bake at 350 degrees for 20 minutes.

Boil lasagna as instructed in box. In a separate pot, mix frozen veggie mix and pasta sauce until hot. Add all seasonings desired. Simmer until frozen veggies thaw.

In a large casserole dish, layer lasagna, eggplant slices, ricotta cheese, shredded cheese, and sauce. Sprinkle cheese on top. Bake at 350 degrees for 45 minutes or until cheese is completely melted at the top.

INEN VERSUS PLASTIC

I guess you must know my opinion on this. Every Diva should own at least 3 Linen table cloths. White, Ivory, Red or Black. Nothing says formal like a Linen tablecloth.

Also it is great when setting up your table for the Holiday Season.

They may be an occasion when you may choose to use Plastic tablecloths. I say when you have a Picnic or outdoor activity or Kids party but when hosting an Adult event choose Linen.

You may find them on sale often, pick them up and store them away for the times when you may need multiples. Also Party Rental Stores rent for a minimum fee, add this to your budget if possible.

***Diva Tip:** When use candles use White or Ivory candles most often with a Vanilla scent.

Cranberry Relish

2 cans of wholeberry cranberry sauce

1 can mandarin oranges (drain)

1 can crushed pineapple (drain)

1 box frozen strawberries in heavy syrup

1 – 8 oz applesauce

Mix all of the ingredients together in a large bowl. Cover in plastic container with lid. Prepare 2 days before Thanksgiving or dressing/stuffing event. No jellied sauce allowed. Serve.

Corn Casserole

Ingredients:

- 1 15 ¼ oz. can whole kernel corn drained
- 1 14 ¾ oz. creamed corn
- 1 Pack Jiffy corn bread
- 1 Cup (8 oz) sour cream
- ½ Stick of butter, melted
- 1 ½ Cups melted cheese

Preparation:

Preheat oven to 350 degrees. Mix in a large bowl corn, jiffy mix, sour cream, and butter. Pour into greased 13 x 9 dish. Bake for 45 minutes until brown

Fish Soup

Ingredients:

- 2 Tsp. butter
- 2 Chicken bouillon cubes
- 4 Tilapia filters – cut into pieces
- ½lb Small scallops
- 1 Large onion, sliced
- 2 Potatoes cut into cubes

- 2 Cups heavy cream (16 oz)
- 2 Cloves of garlic
- ½ Cup of water
- Red pepper flakes
- Garlic Salt

Preparation:

Sauté onion and garlic in butter, add chicken bouillon cubes, ½ cup water, and potatoes. Simmer for 10 minutes. Season fish with garlic salt, add to pan and simmer for 5 minutes. Add heavy cream and red pepper flakes. Taste to make sure it is delicious and the perfect for your taste!

Potato Soup

Ingredients:

- 5 Potatoes, peeled and cubed
- 1 Leek sliced, rinse until clear
- 3 Cloves of garlic pressed (may be used from the jar)
- 2 Chicken bouillon cubes
- 16 oz. heavy cream

- ½ Cup of milk (optional)
- 2 Tsp. salt
- ½ Tsp. pepper
- 1 Cup shredded cheddar cheese
- 1/8 Stick of butter

Preparation:

Peel and rinse potatoes, cut into cubes or desired pieces. Place them in a large sauce pan with water to boil, cook until potatoes are soft (about 30 minutes) and drain. In a sauce pan, sauté leeks in butter, salt, pepper, garlic, and chicken bouillon cubes – break them up. Add potatoes, then heavy cream. Simmer about 15 minutes, add additional milk if needed, and enjoy.

Shredded Cabbage

Ingredients:

- 1 Cabbage sliced super thin
- 1 Bag of carrot sticks (produce dept.)
- 2 Chicken bouillon cubes
- 1 Stick of butter
- Red pepper flakes
- Lemon pepper

Preparation:

Sauté cabbage in large frying pan in butter and chicken bouillon cubes over medium heat. Add carrot sticks, sprinkle with pepper flakes and lemon pepper. Do not over-cook. Cabbage should take about 10 minutes, should be cooked but not limp.

Sweet Potato Pie

1 pie sell, unbaked (9 inch)

1 pound sweet potatoes, baked and peeled

¼ cup butter or margarine

1 can of Sweetened Condensed Milk

1 teaspoon vanilla extract

1 teaspoon cinnamon

1 teaspoon ground nutmeg

2 egg

½ cup brown sugar

Preheat oven to 350 degrees F. In large mixing bowl, beat hot sweet potatoes with butter until smooth. Add remaining ingredients except crust: mix well. Pour into pie shell. Bake 40 minutes or until golden brown. Cool. Garnish as desired

*You can substitute canned pumpkin and make it pumpkin pie

Quickie Peach Cobbler

1 box of Yellow or Pound Cake Mix

1 Large Can of Sliced Peaches in Heavy Syrup

I stick of Margarine or butter- Melted

Pour Peaches in 13 X 9 pan. Sprinkle Cake Mix evenly over peaches, making sure there are no lumps in the mix. Pat down over peaches. Pour melted margarine or butter over cake mixture evenly, making sure evenly covered. Add more if needed for coverage. Bake at 350 degrees until cobbler is golden brown and crusty and syrup bubbles into mix. Serve a la mode

***Diva Tip:** This tastes great. A no fail desert. Serve in a great bowl or dish and you will end meal on a high note.

Apple Walnut Bread Pudding

Ingredients:

- 10 Slices honey wheat bread, crumbled
- 1 Cup walnuts crushed
- 2 Cups dark brown sugar
- 5 Eggs
- 1 Can apple pie filling, chopped coarsely with fork

- 2 Cups heavy whipping cream
- ½ Cup golden raisins
- ¼ Cup butter, softened
- Cinnamon
- Vanilla ice cream (optional)

Preparation:

Preheat oven to 350 degrees. Mix together brown sugar, eggs, milk, and cinnamon. Pour over crumbled bread. Add walnuts, pie filling, raisins, and mix well. Pour into well greased 13 x 9 pan. Bake 30-45 minutes. Cut and serve a la mode, it's the best!

Diva's Can Que'

Hey, I love to Barbeque. I usually use a gas Grill because I can Grill year round.

I especially like Grilling Steaks and Fish. I use my Steak Marinade and Love to serve grilled vegetables with my grill pan the fit right on the grill that prevent burning and too much char.

Suggested Mix:

Red Onions   Mushrooms

Zucchini   Green & Red Peppers

Eggplant

I pre-boil my corn and then finish it on the grill to give it that smokey grilled flavor.

I serve it with a special butter mixture in individual souffle cups.

Butter Mixture:

Softened Butter   Grated Parmesean Cheese

Pressed Garlic   Dried Parley flakes

Great for Adult Barbeques.

GIRL'S NITE OUT

You have worked 50-60 hours this week.

Your CEO, CFO, Adminstrator has worked the last nerve you have left.

You have heard enough about billable hours, budget cuts, and RVUs for one week.

The only cure- GIRL'S NITE OUT

Planning a Girl's Nite out with your Crew can be as Simple as Making a Reservation for Dinner or you may choose something more detailed as a cocktail party at home with a Makeup session or Pole Dancing.

Whatever you Choose, Make the food good. If you do it at home consider a Chef or order the Food from a Restaurant.

******Diva Tip:** Order Food from Restaurants, Delivery Service like Doorstep Delivery will Pick up for Most Restaurants and Deliver to your door. Remember to order at least 1 hour in at advance.

Lutheria Hollis is a Mother, Grandmother and Sisterfriend. She works in Healthcare and lives in Florida. She has Planned and Directed Weddings and many parties and events over the years. The Photos cover photo and inside back cover was taken in her hometown of Havana Florida. Known for their antiques, by Kenni Monae.

Printed in the United States
By Bookmasters